WordPlay

By: Courtney Prudhomme

© 2017 Courtney Prudhomme
All rights reserved.

ISBN: 0692980695
ISBN 13: 9780692980699
LCCN Imprint Name: **Houston, Texas**

Contents

I.	Been a Poet
II.	Risky
III.	Thots Running
IV.	Slippery
V.	No Problems
VI.	Tilted
VII.	Unpredictable
VIII.	Becoming
IX.	Stuck
X.	Residue
XI.	Resilience
XII.	Magnet
XIII.	Space
XIV.	Same Time
XV.	Trips
XVI.	Smoke
XVII.	Hold Up
XVIII.	Like Me
XIX.	Cost Me
XX.	Simple
XXI.	Reality
XXII.	Conditional
XXIII.	Hands Full
XXIV.	Distant and Different
XXV.	Maze
XXVI.	Highway
XXVII.	Don't Deny It
XXVIII.	Tricks on Me
XXIX.	Witness
XXX.	Opportunities
XXXI.	Think I'm Falling
XXXII.	Ash

I. Been a Poet

I've been a poet since the day I was born
I remember the day I had to finally mourn
Like being ripped in pieces, I was feeling torn
Heartbreak from a death is no feeling that's foreign
But I trust the process, I feel the pain
I walk outside, and I feel the rain
My mood switches, and I feel the change
Suppress these thoughts, then I give her brain

II. Risky

Live my life on the edge, I'm risky
Overthinking while life gets tricky
Stuck on you, got me feeling sticky
I'm sick and tired, got me feeling icky
I'm so high until you cannot reach me
I want to have sex until I'm sleepy
When life sucks, come home and freak me
Like a faucet, you got me leaking
Tell the truth because I'm tired of sneaking
I just need something real to believe in
There are some things I would kill to believe in
But my mind is confusing, and my heart is misleading
All the love I gave but didn't receive
To prove my love, I don't need receipts
Last night you were on top of me
Thoughts of you are locked in me
When I'm committed, there's no stopping me
I'm the best, that's the god in me
Heartbreak has hardened me
But my emotions are a part of me
Live my life on the edge, I'm risky
Overthinking while life gets tricky
Stuck on you, got me feeling sticky
I'm sick and tired, got me feeling icky

III.   Thots Running

Thoughts running
Thots running
Using words just for wordplay
Love birds on a playdate
I'm so high, I sit and watch the birds play
She became my weak-end like a Saturday
I'm so charged up like a battery
Smiling at the flattery, she tatted me
Studying my pedigree, I'm here to stay
Turning all these lemons into lemonade
Nonbeliever, I went renegade
I just move up, and I get a raise
I'm not here to play
I'm not here to praise
I know I got the juice like Minute Maid
I know I got the juice like lemonade
My bars are sick, it needs mental aid

IV. Slippery

Emotions feeling slippery
I fell for you, no injury
You got me weak, no energy
All I have are memories
Loyalty is limiting
No melody, no symphony
Commitment and liberty
I just want some lemon tea
Fed my misery
Now I'm gone, you're missing me
Look at how you bend for me
Messages being sent to me
It's the way I deliver me
Drop you like delivery
No one in this world can hinder me
I fell for you, no injury

V.   No Problems

I don't want no problems
Said the message in the bottle
I don't sit down for this
I'm standing like a model
Sipping on moscato
Truth is hard to swallow
Zoning out my sorrows
Hard for me to follow
Walk into tomorrow
This time that I borrow
I don't want no problems
Plus, I'm tired and my eyes low

VI. Tilted

I know it's not Thanksgiving
But I'm thankful
You're alive and living
Drinking lemonade when life throws me lemons
When I'm down on my luck, I'm in the clouds getting lifted
Every day my mind is shifting, far away I feel I'm drifting
Live my life in the present, I recognize that I'm gifted
Recognize that I'm different, recognize that I've shifted
And did it all while lifted
Body leaning, I'm tilted

VII.   Unpredictable

I'm unpredictable
I move like tentacles
The way I think and feel are identical
I'm kind of cynical
I think too deep, I'm critical
Don't take it so literal
But the one thing to be true is my love so beautiful

VIII.   Becoming

Tell me what's becoming
I'm down for you, I'm cuming
Stick to you like honey
Rubbing on my tummy
Tell me that you love me
Hold on to me, hug me
I can tell you want to fuck me
Got me feeling lucky
Body's hot like it's the summer
Feeling soft, it makes you ponder
How I'm tensed and feel like thunder
Body long like anaconda
I just want to get up under
I just want to feel the thunder
I just want to feel the summer
All I do is feel and wonder
Crave you and I feel the hunger
Fuck you in my brand-new Honda
Make love until the sun's up
Then plan a trip to London
I think about you, it's redundant
Now you're leaving, now I'm coming
Butterflies in my stomach
About to drive thru like Sonic
I miss you, and I'm being honest
Feel the time has come, You're running
Tell me what's becoming

IX. Stuck

Stuck in my mind
Fuck with my time
Fuck up the journey
Switch up my lines
And I was in a hurry
Now it's slowing up my grind
Blinded by the shine
When I open up the blinds
Life is on my back like a spine
Touching my brain
No wonder why it's fucking with my mind
Life cuts me deep on my wrist like the time
I want things to change like a dime

X. Residue

I remember how I fucked you like an animal
And left residue on the sheets
More residue on my cheeks
Left residue on my sleeve
Saw residue on my feet
Then saw you in my dreams
We didn't even speak

XI. Resilience

This is life
It keeps me liable
But writing poetry every day keeps me viable
Consistent like reliable
Life is not a pot of gold
Reach another downward slope
Makes me climb the rope
Falling like a domino
Now I have to float
My thoughts run like water
Now I have to flow
Life is on the boat
I'm hanging by a rope
Inhale the breeze
Exhale the smoke

XII.   Magnet

She told me I was attractive
Then became attracted like a magnet
I guess loving me is a habit
To be honest, I am past it
Only some shit is forever
Everything's not everlasting
Some things are plastic
At times you won't know it
Until you have it
Body language speaking Spanish
Crushed like a can is
Soft like the sand is, touching like a hand is
So gone it's like I vanished, so high I'm not landing
Shit gets real, organic
Life is full of chances
I'm from another planet
Ease my mind when I panic
Only way to manage
I have to understand it
I have to take advantage
When I feel hypomanic
I am fucking candid
I don't mean to be outlandish
I don't let my thoughts get stranded
I sink like the Titanic

XIII. Space

If you need some space
I'm high like the moon
The scent of our sex
On my neck like perfume
The clock hits twelve
It's finally noon
Try to be the one
Before the clock moves
Thinking to myself
I have to hit snooze
I can't take it if I lose
Time is moving forward
And I'm running out of room
Get a little closer, I want to spoon
When life cuts me deep like a knife
Sweep me off my feet like a broom

XIV.   Same Time

Last night you were on my mind
But when I wake up, it's the same time
The same shit is on my mind
My life is a movie, and I press rewind
Moving on, getting left behind
I fall like the leaves
Love leaves me blind
I'm just trying to lead my way
But each time I follow my heart
I'm not depressed, I'm just feeling gray
Life is short, can't be here to stay
And that breaks my heart, press pause
But to live for the moment, press play
If love is a game, let's press play
We're both trying to win
For the better, for each other
Because the world, so cold
No sweater
I have no words, like no letters
Thinking of ways I can love better
Write out my heart like a love letter

XV. Trips

She asked me why I look taller
I said, "It's probably 'cause I'm high"
So far off the ground, I'm in the sky
The weather outside got me feeling blah
Feeling bland
Now I'm on the ceiling like a fan
My thoughts expand
'Cause my words play like a band
I got a sense of touch like a hand
I give you 50/50 like a chance
I don't understand
Wrapped around your finger like a band
More than a crush, like a can
Chilling on the beach like the sand
Pick up my world, and I put it in my hands
I pick up my girl, and I put her in my hands
It's like I picked up my life and put it in the van
Trip and trip, it's like I'm hanging from a cliff
Trip after trip, I hope I never land

XVI. Smoke

Been like six months since I last wrote
But half a second since I smelled smoke
Mind like flowers, I see the growth
I'm in the sky, feels like a boat
My thoughts are wavy, and I begin to float
Thoughts flow like water, try not to soak
All these bars got me dripping like soap
Life is a slippery slope
I'm so blunt, they think I'm dope
Gone like the wind, it continues to blow
I'm all in the air, you would think I'm smoke
Thoughts so cold, I need a coat
Pass it to me like childhood notes
Life's tug-of-war, got to pull the rope
The way I think makes my mind shiver
Thoughts flow like the Nile River

XVII. Hold Up

Hold up, I just had to speak
Been thinking about it for about a week
Been a long time since I fell asleep
Since you left, I've been deep
Smoke in the air, I don't drink
Sometimes I feel and I don't think
The waves get rough, and I start to sink
Then I open my eyes, I start to blink
High as the clouds
I'm high as a peak
Sober thoughts
I'm high as a tree
Rolling thoughts
While I'm high as a bee
I get high as a leap
These sober thoughts won't put me to sleep
So when I saw you, I just had to speak
It's been a minute now, about a week
So hold up, I just had to speak

XVIII. Like Me

Apparently
I have a bad bitch who looks like me
She has a bad bitch who looks like her
She has me softer than fur
First thing I do is
I take off her shirt
She already knows
It's all about her
All about us
I don't need to rehearse
Moving forward, no need to reverse
She's bad as fuck
And I want to fuck
Out all my sorrows
'Cause life sucks
And apparently
I'm in her fantasy
I'm on top
Like a canopy
So calm, like the sand and sea
I'm hearing things that I cannot see
That I have a bad bitch who looks like me

XIX. Cost Me

What you did really cost me
What you did really lost me
Now you got my heart exhausted
Like you grabbed my heart
And you tossed it
Mind keeps running like a faucet
Mind moves fast, I got to pause it
Cupid throwing arrows, dodge it
Shooting shots, can't be the target
Rubbed me wrong, no massages
Sit and think, what really caused it?
Sit and watch as it's demolished
Heart in my pocket like a wallet
Give me four years like a college
I'm in the sky, like a pilot
I put in, like a deposit
I give it to her, no deposit

XX. Simple

Why does it have to be so difficult,
When it can all be so simple?
Why do I feel it all breaking?
I just want it to be all mental
Write it down in ink, it's permanent
Why can't it be in all pencil?
So we can erase the bullshit and start over
If only it were that simple

XXI. Reality

Fuck reality and its bad creation
I live in this world for recreation
Life is a fucking joke
Fuck reality
I'm losing hope
Fuck reality
I'm about to smoke
Fuck reality
Fuck reality
I'm about to float
Fuck this world
Like it's for show
I'm so high, I'll need a pole
My mind strips, and it's time to roll
Like tug-of-war, I'll need a rope
Like a turtle, I'm moving slow
So fucking raw, I'm so fucking dope
Fuck reality and all its hoes

XXII. Conditional

It's conditional
Sometimes I need a visual
Like a video
In the ceiling when I'm feeling low
Feeling pitiful
I'm original
I'm here for growth
Please tell me something that I didn't know
Too much on my mind, I have to leave a note
I just want to lick you like an envelope

XXIII. Hands Full

So down for you, I never left you
My love is permanent like a tattoo
Start over, make everything brand-new
Three years' worth of memories I ran through
Somebody please tell me what I can't do
She's crushing on me like a can do
I'm burning for you like a candle
You're nothing that I can't handle
And that ass keeps my hands full
You say I can be a handful
But I'm the truth, no scandal

XXIV. Distant and Different

Lately, we're distant and different
Nothing lasts forever, can be taken from me
in an instant
I just want to write so I can pass the minutes
Sometimes I don't even feel like I'm really
living
Don't want the lemonade when life throws
me lemons
It's hard to listen
I just need someone to massage this tension
Sometimes I find myself in my head
reminiscing
Before we were
Distant and different

XXV. Maze

Her mind is a maze
Her mind is amazing
I feel like I'm going through a phase
While she's going through all these changes
My mind is everywhere, somewhere in a different place
I'm out of room, I'm out of space
Feels like I'm in a different state
Can't even look you in your face
You would think it was a race
I'm walking at a faster pace
So many thoughts I need to paint
Feeling empty like a blank
I withdraw just like a bank
I can never be a saint
Bars around me like a gate
Emotions stick to me like tape
Got me bluer than a lake
Her mind is a maze
Yet her mind is amazing

XXVI. Highway

Now you feel alone
That shit is funny
I'm not sweet anymore
I'm not honey
If I would've stayed
I would've been a dummy
Now you love me?
Hear your heart growling
Like a tummy
Now you're hungry
How can you be so cold
When it's sunny?
I'm running
Flipping the tables
Turning
Like candles, I'm burning
The hard way, I'm learning
It's either your way or the highway

XXVII. Don't Deny It

It's over like a bridge
No longer can you cross me
I threw in the towel
Before you tried to toss me
Feelings leak like a faucet
I'm high like a rocket
I just want to write
Got words in my pocket
I'm the plug like a socket
Heart hopping
I'm a drug
You're an addict, popping
You're here for the wrong reason
Stop it

I know what I want, and I got it
My feelings, I never hide it
Used to put my tongue inside it
Looking all erotic
It's obvious, I still love you
I don't deny it

XXVIII. Tricks on Me

My mind is playing tricks on me
And now you want to lick on me
And now you want to kiss on me
Got my mind playing tricks on me
Hard to choose who was sent for me
I don't know who was meant for me
I just want it all to make sense to me
My mind is playing tricks on me

XXIX. Witness

Things change and make no sense
Emotion blue like an ocean
Situation's ashy, no lotion
Take a trip to Mars, I'm floating
I can't feel a thing, I'm frozen
Red plants around me, roses
I'm lit, I think I'm exploding
Fuck shit up like an erosion
I go through life like a rodent
I'm laid out on a rug
Thoughts flying like a bug
Watch my bars turn to suds
Now I'm wet like a tub
Handshakes turn to hugs
It's all relative, like blood
Witness hard times turn to mud
Witness "hate yous" turn to love

XXX. Opportunities

Opportunities that I'm glad I missed
I told her goodbye without a kiss
Try to be on top like I'm a lid
Words filthy, I talk shit
Mind is gone, I lost it
Got me high like a mountain
Get me wet like a fountain
Ticktock, where the time went?
I eat you out, then we dine in
My wordplay is so childish

XXXI.   Think I'm falling

I can see my dreams
I can see my visions
I was moving slow
Moved a couple of inches
Trapped in indecision
Cut me like an incision
Same shit but feels different
Guess we just see different
 I think I love you
I think I'm tripping
I think I'm falling
I think I'm slipping
I'm on a mission
And I miss you
But I think I love you
I think I'm tripping
I'm feeling clumsy
I think I'm slipping

XXXII.   Ash

Memories of you have me painting pictures in my head
I don't even draw, but I'm painting pictures in my bed
You didn't walk, instead you cut me deep when you fled
We didn't talk, now I have no heart, now I'm dead
From the start, my heart has been in conflict with my head
With us apart, I have all these feelings that I dread

The End

Available from Amazon.com and other retailers

www.ingramcontent.com/pod-product-compliance
Lightning Source LLC
Chambersburg PA
CBHW021002090426
42736CB00010B/1422